T0064238

Amelia Island

BOOK OF SECRETS

MARITIME ARCHAEOLOGIST SCOTT R. JENSEN M.A.

authorHOUSE

AuthorHouse™
1663 Liberty Drive
Bloomington, IN 47403
www.authorhouse.com
Phone: 833-262-8899

© 2021 Maritime Archaeologist Scott R. Jensen M.A. All rights reserved.

No part of this book may be reproduced, stored in a retrieval system, or transmitted by any means without the written permission of the author.

Published by AuthorHouse 03/19/2021

ISBN: 978-1-6655-1521-4 (sc)
ISBN: 978-1-6655-1527-6 (e)

Library of Congress Control Number: 2021901436

Print information available on the last page.

Any people depicted in stock imagery provided by Getty Images are models, and such images are being used for illustrative purposes only.
Certain stock imagery © Getty Images.

This book is printed on acid-free paper.

Because of the dynamic nature of the Internet, any web addresses or links contained in this book may have changed since publication and may no longer be valid. The views expressed in this work are solely those of the author and do not necessarily reflect the views of the publisher, and the publisher hereby disclaims any responsibility for them.

DEDICATION

It is a pleasure in writing this book to acknowledge the cooperation of my artifact hunting teammates; Matt Batten, Don Gay, William L. Taylor, and Candi Nichols, who have shared the same drive for hunting artifacts as myself.

I also want to acknowledge Noël Marie Lehman who encouraged me to write this book. Lastly and so importantly, I also want to acknowledge my parents whom I love dearly.

CONTENTS

INTRODUCTION

This book is not intended to be an earth-shattering novel divulging the secrets of all treasure; it is simply an educational book entitled, *Amelia Island Book of Secrets*.

The island is rich in archaeological sites, and to date there are over 65 on record. Most archaeological sites do not translate into treasure. However, that being said, I will concentrate on some of the treasure sites (and one archaeological site) on Amelia Island located in Nassau County Florida.

The public assumes no treasure has been found on Amelia Island. Some believe there was never any treasure on the island; believe the author, they are **wrong**. I shall go into a brief history of Amelia Island and this will help the reader to understand where the island is located. Chapters 3-9 will concentrate on the details of treasure sites of Amelia Island.

⊁ CHAPTER ONE ⊱

History of Amelia Island

AMELIA ISLAND, FLORIDA IS KNOWN as the *Isle of Eight Flags*, and with good reason. Eight flags have flown over this island. The French, the Spanish, the British, the Patriots, the Green Cross, the Mexican Republic, the Confederate and lastly the United States flag. This is not intended to be a publication on the history of the island, but is merely a review of the history to let readers know where Amelia Island is located and what secrets it holds. You will be able to understand where you are, by going through this Island's past.

According to *Environmental Geology Series*, Amelia Island lies at 30.62' North 81.46' West. The island is 4 miles in width and 13.5 miles in length. Amelia Island was formed from river deposited alluvium that was piled up by wind, ocean, and storms.

According to *Yesterday's Reflections* the French Huguenot leader, Jean Ribault, who landed on the island in 1562, recorded the first contact with Europeans in the Amelia Island area. Ribault named it the *Isle de Mai* (Island of May) (Johannes 2000). Although the Spanish had originally claimed La Florida for their empire, this did not prevent the French from trying and succeeding to break the Spanish hold on this part of the New World. Spain had claimed the area in 1513, however, that did not prevent the French colonists from landing.

Colonists were not only seeking land for France, but also refuge from religious and political persecution. Though Ribault and his company didn't remain, the Huguenots returned again in 1564 under the leadership of René de Laudonniere, who was a commander on another return voyage (Amelia Island Museum of History 2009).

According to *The European Discovery of America*, the second colony constructed Fort Caroline in north eastern Florida in 1562. Spanish troops led by Pedro Menéndez de Aviles slaughtered these French settlers in order to regain the territory the Spanish had claimed in previous years (Morison 1974).

According to *The Indians of Amelia Island*, the first Spanish reign was from 1565 to 1763. The Timucuan numbers started to decline due to the influx of European disease and the disruption of their lifestyle. Though the Timucuan numbers were once 30,000, they were almost completely extinct within about 100 years of their first contact with the Europeans (Jaccard 2000).

According to the *Florida Archaeology*, the British settlements in the north took an interest in the area because of the naturally deep ports and the strategic trade route location. Georgia's Governor James Oglethorpe named the island "Amelia" in 1735 in honor of Princess Amelia, daughter of King George II.

Though the British named the Island Amelia, it did not fall into British hands until Spanish Florida was traded for British Cuba in 1763. During the time of British rule, which lasted until 1783, the island was known as Egmont.

In 1783, the Second Treaty of Paris ended the French Revolutionary War and returned Florida to Spain. British inhabitants of Florida had to leave the province within 18 months unless they swore allegiance to Spain. In 1811, surveyor George J. F. Clarke platted the town "Fernandina" who had chosen the name in honor of King Ferdinand VII of Spain.

To drive out the Spanish, the Patriots of Amelia Island, an independent group of American civilians backed by the United States government, seized control of the island and raised their flag on March 17, 1812.

The next day, the Patriots ceded Amelia Island to the United States. However, Spain's strong protest forced the U.S. to relinquish its new possession, especially in light of the impending War of 1812 with England.

In 1817, a Scotsman named Sir Gregor MacGregor, with the support of some key Americans, ran the Spanish off the island and raised the Green Cross of Florida flag. However, because of lack of reinforcements and funds, MacGregor left the island and his lieutenants took charge.

These lieutenants made a deal with Frenchman Luis Aury (a soldier in the Mexican Revolution) in order to gain support to maintain control. However, Aury, in return for giving them support, wanted to command the island and therefore raised the Mexican Republic flag.

According to *Florida Archaeology* the town came into such a state of bedlam that the U.S. government sent gunboats, took control, and held Amelia Island in trust for Spain until Florida became a U.S. territory on July 10, 1821 (Fairbanks and Mcanich 1980).

According to *Fort Clinch*, the Confederates took control of Fort Clinch, which had been started by the Federals and later abandoned because of the outbreak of the Civil War. The Confederate flag was raised at Fort Clinch in April 1861. In less than a year, Union forces surrounded the Fort, and Union control held throughout the remainder of the war (Gooding 1974).

In the time period from 1870 to 1910, many wealthy Americans made their home on Amelia Island. In New Fernandina they constructed elegant Victorian style homes. The boom was due to the shipping industry and the fact that many New Yorkers were coming down by steamboat to enjoy the climate. In 1890, Standard Oil co-founder Henry Flagler opened up the railroad in Florida and detoured much of the tourist traffic to St. Augustine and places further south.

Flagler's actions resulted in a faltering local economy on Amelia Island until some local fishermen saw the potential in the area for netting shrimp. This industry was started on Amelia Island in the early 1900s. Subsequently, two paper mills were also located on the island, which provided an additional boost to the economy.

In the 1970's, Amelia Island Plantation and the Ritz-Carlton were built as a resort with a natural setting. This resulted in the island being recognized as a tourist area.

⚜ CHAPTER TWO ⚜

Pirates!

SOME PEOPLE THINK THAT NASSAU County, Florida is associated with Nassau in the Bahamas (a pirate hangout); it is not (Nassau County was named for the Duchy / Duchess of Nassau in Germany). People surmise that's why pirates were on Amelia Island; it is not.

There were pirates on the island because it was a lawless area and it was the deepest natural port on the east coast, so with that combination; pirates flocked to the island!

The most famous pirates in the vicinity of Amelia Island in what I would call the **First Pirates Period** 1680-1763 were as follows: Captain William Kidd, Blackbeard, Calico Jack Rackham, Mary Read, Anne Bonny, Abraham Agramont, Red Legs Greaves, Montbars (The Exterminator), and Henry Morgan.

Captain William Kidd, or as he was called by the people; Captain Kidd. Kidd was a familiar Privateer on Amelia Island. A Privateer was sanctioned by a particular country to attack other countries' ships. (A Privateer is similar to a Buccaneer).

Captain Kidd was said to have a fortune in gold and silver hidden on Amelia, in several locations around the island. In Chapter 5, you will read about an unknown number of expeditions that were on Amelia Island. These were published in newspapers in 1935; the expeditions where strictly designed to find Kidd's and Aury's treasure. (Although I suspect any treasure would do).

According to *The Book of Pirates Treasures,* Captain Kidd was decreed by England to attack French ships, and that was when his troubles started. Kidd attacked a ship that was flying a French flag. To his dismay, it had a captain from England. Captain Kidd was captured and charged with piracy (some say he turned himself in) in Massachusetts in July 1699.

Kidd was transported to London, England to face his charges. After much deliberation, he was sentenced to hang. Thousands of people turned out for his execution. He was hanged in May 1701. Amazingly, the rope broke; but fear not, Kidd was hanged successfully on the second try. Kidd's body was placed in a gibbet (a type of cage) and hung over the harbor as a warning to other pirates. Captain William Kidd's reign lasted approximately from the late 1600's to his execution in 1701.

The second historically important pirate is Edward Teach; you may know him as Blackbeard. The pirate was known to hang out on Amelia Island on many occasions. When he was not in Nassau, the pirate would stop on Amelia Island before going on to the Carolinas

After grounding the *Queen Anne's Revenge* near what is now known as Beaufort, North Carolina (some people think he grounded it purposely others think not) and switched it to a faster ship. Blackbeard continued his plundering until his death.

According to *Republic of Pirates,* Lieutenant Robert Maynard killed Teach in

1718; he decapitated Blackbeard and hung his head from the bow of his ship. Blackbeard's reign of terror lasted from 1716-1718.

The next pirates that are important to discuss will include Calico Jack Rackham, Anne Bonny and Mary Read. The old-timers say they walked around on Amelia Island. The famous pirate Rackham, met Anne Bonny in Nassau and the two got married. Rackham, along with Anne Bonny and Mary Read (Mary Read and Anne Bonny were also well-known pirates) were captured together.

Calico Jack Rackham was sentenced to death in 1720 however, Read and Bonny were both with child. During that time period, they would not execute a woman who was pregnant. Mary Read died in prison and Anne Bonny disappeared from the prison and was never seen in the Nassau (Bahamas) area again.

Calico Jack Rackham died in 1720; his reign as a pirate lasted from 1718 - 1720. Anne Bonny's reign as a pirate lasted from 1718 – unknown. Mary Read tenure was from 1708-1721.

The last pirate in what I call the **First Pirate Period** was Abraham Agramont. I cannot verify Red Legs Greaves, Montbars, or Henry Morgan were ever on Amelia Island, however, I thought I would include them and let the readers and future treasure hunters sort that out.

According to *The Enslavement of the American Indian in the Colonial Times* Agramont was a ruthless pirate, with a take no prisoner attitude. He scorched the coast from Georgia to Amelia Island and down as far as St. Augustine. The pirate was unsuccessful at burning St Augustine (Olexer: P 110). Agramont had a soft spot for missions.

I surmise that the pirate had spared the lives of the missionaries, as Agramont moved them to Amelia Island and Talbot Island. He used Amelia Island to set up a camp that the Spanish called *Santa Maria*.

The Second Pirate Period on Amelia Island was in the time period of 1784-1817 and included Jean Lafitte and Luis Aury. I can't confirm that Lafitte was actually on Amelia Island. He was a West Coast pirate, who made a deal to pardon his crew and himself with General Andrew Jackson. He accepted and was involved in the Battle of New Orleans. I have no idea if he was on the island. However, according to *Seeing Fernandina*, one woman in the 1800's said she had an encounter with Lafitte.

The next pirate discussed will be Luis Aury. Aury took control of Amelia Island in September 1817 and was forced out by Union troops in December 1817. His tenure on Amelia Island was short; four months. He was a pirate who took control of the island with Gregor MacGregor.

According to documents located in *The Maritime Museum of Amelia Island Archives*, Aury established a pirate's town called *Aurytown* (Talbot Island). In 2020, Archaeologists found a Timucuan Indian village with European pottery on Talbot Island. This may be the location of *Aurytown;* on top of the Indian village. I can tell you with certainty that nothing remains of that town.

Prizes were seized ships by pirates. During his reign, there were as many as eight prizes in the port at one time. Aury's real wealth came from seizing slave ships and selling the slaves in Georgia. He was born in France in 1788 and died in 1821.

Figure 1

CHAPTER THREE

Old Fernandina / New Fernandina

T HIS WAS TAKEN FROM THE original *Amelia Island Book of Secrets* that I wrote after 25 years of exploration, treasure hunting and talking to people; but never published. Notice on the map above, New Fernandina is located in the confines of the area south of Old Fernandina. On the map provided by *The Maritime Museum of Amelia Island Archives* Figure 1, there were very few roads on the island. Today, there are approximately 2000 roads on Amelia Island.

A massive boardwalk through the marshlands connected Old Fernandina and New Fernandina. There was no road access going to Old Fernandina. According to *Yesterday Reflections,* the map in Figure 2 shows Old Fernandina and New Fernandina connected through the marshlands by a boardwalk.

Figure 2

This area is now called Old Town; at one time it was called Old Fernandina. Figure 3 is a map drawn in the original *Book of Secrets*; the map was from 1821 with updates from other maps circa 1784.

I personally visited with several residents from Old Town. Many of the residents had dug up coquina steps underground, seeming to go nowhere. Supposedly the steps led to a tunnel with the purpose of residents escaping to Fort San Carlos. Many people believe the tunnel is under Egan's Creek, as an archaeologist, I can assure you that is not possible.

Figure 4 shows a cross on the ground near the main gate. Figure 4 & 5 will explain why and how it was constructed. (The Figures 4 & 5 are identical in nature; however, I was told my writing is horrendous). The cross does not exist today; construction workers found it in early 1800's.

At the time, construction workers were designing and building what is now known as North 14th Street. This project ultimately gave the first civilian road access to Old Town (Old Fernandina).

Figure 3

A map of Old Town

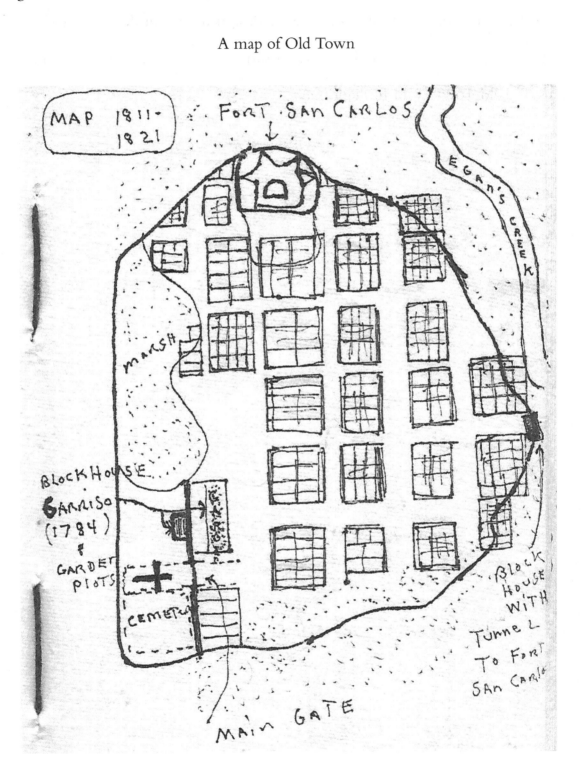

Fragments of the City Gates

Figure 4

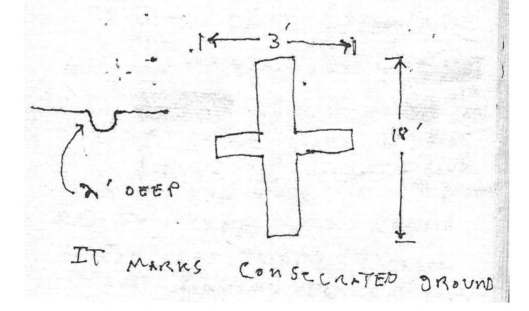

Fragments of the City Gates

Figure 5

- City Gates: Fragments of the foundation are visible. During the building of 14th Street, street workmen unearth a trench in the form of a cross, 18 feet long, 3 feet wide, and filled with oyster shell. 2 feet deep.

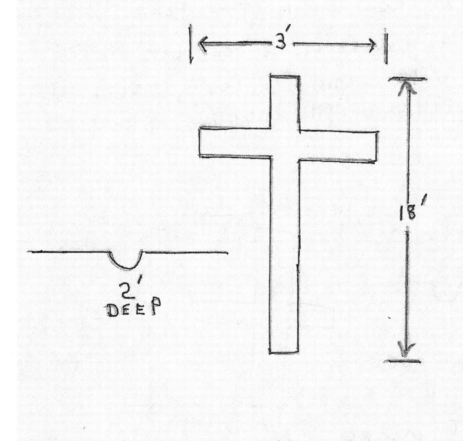

It marks consecrated ground.

Egan's Creek & surrounding areas

Figure 6

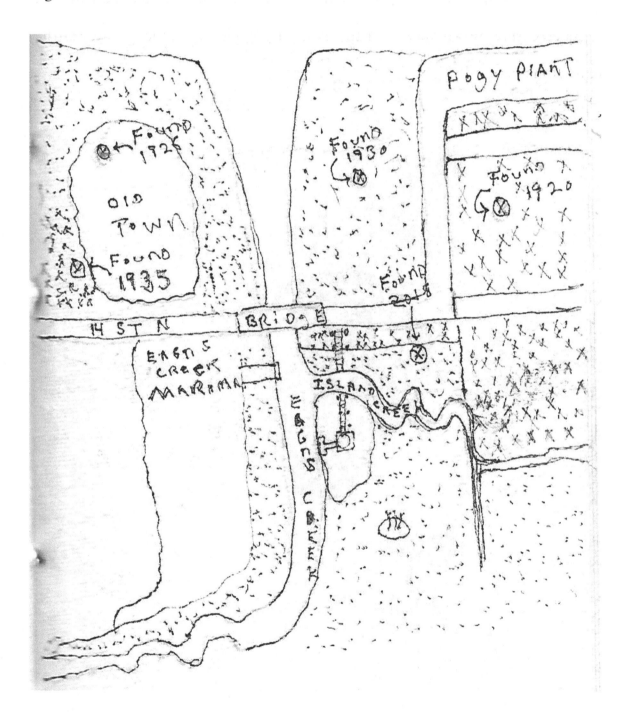

These series of photos are of a coin that was found in Old Fernandina (Old Town). The coin depicts King Ferdinand VII who died in 1833. Old Fernandina, as stated earlier, was named after this King. Look closely at the pictures of the coin as the date is 1833.

Figure 6.1

Figure 6.3

Figure 6.4

CHAPTER FOUR

Treasure!

TREASURE HAS ALWAYS BEEN IN Old Town and the surrounding areas; on numerous occasions coins have been unearthed. According to an *Unknown Text* (partial text) surmised to be from the early 1950's, in 1920 a gentleman named Tray found a pot of silver coins near Fort Clinch.

In 1926, another man found an old can of silver coins at Fort San Carlos. He then took the proceeds and purchased a house on the West Coast of Florida.

In the early thirties (1930's), two men found a cache of gold coins between Old Town and Fort Clinch. There were 400 coins in all, dating back as far as the 1500's. They were of Spanish, French and English coinage.

An inventory of all the coins they found is listed on the following page. This find is impressive...

- Spanish Double Excellentes (1500's)

- French (1600)

- Spanish Double Ducats (1560's)

- French Double Louis (1644)

- English (1640's)

400 coins is a very impressive find from the 1500's to mid-1600's.

In another occurrence approximately five years later, a child was making mud pies near Bosque Bello Cemetery (translated in Spanish as Beautiful Woods) and discovered coins.

Her father came out of the house and helped the child dig the hole. The youngster had uncovered a Spanish pot with $18,000.00 of silver coins in it. This find was made in 1935, and discovered in Old Fernandina.

In 2018, a cache of treasure coins was found in a chest in the Old Town area. I sought out the person who found the cache and located the successful treasure hunter. He took me to a vault location that I will keep secret. I physically touched the case and its' contents. I was amazed at what I was looking at. I was looking into the face of history.

He stated that when the chest was pulled out of the ground, it crumbled. All was not lost; he glued the chest together as best as he could. There was no hardware on the chest; no hinges, no skeleton key hardware and no pins to hold it together.

This treasure hunter would not allow me to photograph the chest, and as a successful archaeologist myself, I do not blame him. This treasure finder was smart. It would bring undo attention to his amazing find, and people may try to claim it.

He, however, allowed me to conduct a quick inventory of the chest and it contained beautiful pieces. It contained gold coins, silver coins, rings, emeralds and gold nuggets. It contained a bronze crucifix, which I found interesting, as it was crafted surprisingly in design with the head of a Mayan / Incan / Aztec style. All the coins were from the 1500's to the 1700's. This is what I saw...................

- 2 Silver Rings

- 2 Gold Doubloons

- 23 Gold Nuggets

- 2 Emeralds

- 119 Silvers Coins

- 1 Crucifix

- 2 Containers

- 1 Chest Wood with skeleton key hole. Disintegrated upon pulling it out of the ground.

Assume the chest is 1700's?

I was very appreciative of the gentleman for allowing me to physically examine his treasure.

Included in this section of **Treasure!** are newspaper articles of more treasures found on the island. According to *The New York Times* published May 28 1897, another man found treasure on Amelia Island. In fact, different groups had discovered $45,000.00 in two finds of Spanish gold.

Several people were in a group looking for the treasure. This individual followed them to their treasure cache and took their map and charts as they slept. Supposedly they could not find the site again and vacated the island.

This individual then took the maps and charts and found what they all had been looking for. He found the treasure containing over $39,000.00 in Spanish gold. The newspaper reported "amateur treasure hunters" dug up four acres at or around the base of multiple trees on the island.

Can you imagine finding a cache of $39,000.00 in 1897? Amelia Island had many plantations on it. The 1897 salary was based on a farmer's salary. The average monthly income was $19.00. According to *Measuring Worth*, the treasure would be worth well over a $1,000, 000.00 in today's value!

This article was taken from the *News-Leader*, which was first published in 1854. It is recognized as the oldest weekly newspaper in Florida. This article was published on October 31,1924.

Figure 7 describes a gentleman who found the coins on Amelia Island. This started a gold rush on the island with people digging on the island with picks and shovels. Like others who preceded him, his treasure find was discovered in Old Town (Old Fernandina).

Figure 7

DISCOVERY OF GOLD NEAR FERNANDINA SETS FOLKS TO WORK WITH SHOVELS AND PICKS

NEGRO FISHERMAN UNEARTHS QUANTITY OF SPANISH DOUBLOONS MINTED MORE THAN 100 YEARS AGO.

The following from the Nassau County Leader tells an interesting story, linking Florida with the early doings of the Spanish buccaneers. It reads:

That fishermen at times have luck ashore, as well as at sea, is proved by the fact that Robt. Cribb, colored, of the shrimp boat "Republic," owned by Frank Graham, of Fernandina, has recently been exhibiting ancient Spanish silver coins which he found on this island last week.

Fisherman Cribb, who lives at Old Town, brought some coins to Mr. Graham last Saturday and asked as to their identity and probable value, stating that the recent heavy rains have washed down a bank near Old Town and that he dug the coins out at the edge of the cavern.

Those he exhibited to Mr. Graham were of silver and a trifle larger than our U. S. silver dollar but not quite as thick, and they probably contain about the same amount of silver as the U. S. dollar.

One of the coins is dated 1796 and has on its face a likeness of Carolus Fourth, King of Spain. Others bear the likeness of Ferdinand Seventh, king of Spain. All the coins are over a hundred years old and still they show no signs of hard usage. All the letters of the inscriptions on both the obverse and reverse sides of the money are as plain and easily read as when they were minted. Also they are almost as bright and untarnished as when new.

The freshman who found them is not communicative as to how many he secured, nor will he state definitely where the caved bank is located, except to say that it is near Old Town, and not far from Fort Clinch. No one blames him for his reticence. The find is his find.

Members of old-time families now resident at Old Town tell tales handed down to them from their great-grandparents, of how Amelia Island was, a hundred years ago, a famous rendezvous for the pirates of the Spanish Main, and they will to this day show visitors the rotted timbers of an ancient dock at Old Town where they say their ancestors claimed the pirates made their landings. Has Fisherman Cribb found buried pirate treasure or is the money a relic of the Spanish occupation of this island?

The coins are too bright and too nearly "mint proof" to have been carelessly lost by some one. Their fine condition leads to the inference that they had been carefully packed away.

Cribb gave one of the older coins to his employer, Mr. Frank Graham, who brought it to the Leader office for exhibition to any one interested.

The news of this find has aroused once more the ambition of the many Ferdinand treasure hunters who are wise to the fact that one fortune in gold doubloons

In speaking with the old-timers, they often spoke of another treasure from the late 1800's. It was a story in which three men were on the hunt with a map. According to the old-timers one man died and the other two men continued on.

The group told me that the two men found a hole in the back of "The Creek" (Egan's Creek, perhaps?) and more treasure is still there. The story goes that the two remaining men found $170,000.00 in gold and jewels. The Port of Call for the vessel that transported the treasure was New York.

Finding $170,000.00 in gold and silver the treasure would be worth roughly $4,000,000.00 dollars today. The author cannot confirm this, but Amelia Island has many stories like this!

Figures 8 and 9 are of a letter sent to the *Fernandina Chamber of Commerce* describing a lady's search for treasure on Amelia Island.

Figure 8

February 3, 1934.

Dear Madam:

Your letter of January 29th addressed to the Postmaster of Fernandina, Florida, has been referred to us for reply.

During the period from 1680 to 1763 Cumberland Sound and Amelia River was a harbor of rendezvous for slave traders and pirates. In 1763 the peninsular of Florida was ceded, by Spain, to England and under English rule this lawless element did not find favorable operating conditions, hence they abandoned the use of the harbor. In 1784 the peninsular was ceded back to Spain and from then on until 1817 was again a favorite harbor for free booters. During these two periods it has been assumed that treasure was buried by pirates on the Island. We do not know of any actual instance of treasure having been found except that in 1928 or 1929 a small quantity of ancient coins were turned up during excavation.

In the neighborhood of the beach is a long narrow stretch of hammock land and on this tract an old negro lived for many years, named Uncle Jimmie Drummond. He was called a Seminole Indian but long time residents here say he was a full blooded negro. He was, however, a very unique character. He habitually kept a pen of rattle snakes and had a reputation among the colored people here of being able to conjure. The legend is that somewhere on the tract of land on which he lived there was buried treasure and that near that treasure was an oak tree with an old iron chain hanging in the tree and grown into it. The legend further states that on dark nights the chain will be rattled by spirit hands and no one had the courage to excavate for this treasure for fear of death at the hands of these guardian spirits. Uncle Jimmie died last year.

Figure 9

Early last year we had a caller in this office who mentioned these stories of hidden treasures and who stated that he had authentic information of the location of some of this treasure and was planning on coming over here some dark night and digging it up for removal. He, of course, would not divulge the location of this treasure and stated that if he did dig it up no one would ever know about it because he did not intend that the owner of the land should claim any of the treasure.

All of these stories are very interesting but so far as we know no treasure of any quantity, except a few ancient coins, has ever been dug up.

We trust this will give you the information requested in your letter.

Yours very truly,

Secretary.
FERNANDINA CHAMBER OF COMMERCE.

RAS/w

Cy -

Gold Rush in New Fernandina

A cache of gold bars was found at a site in New Fernandina in 1976. According to the Fernandina Beach Court House (which displays one of the bars), it caused so much commotion in the city that they dispatched the police to guard the find.

People were raiding the site as the word of the find spread around the town. Treasure hunters and civilians alike were coming into the city with shovels, pick axes and whatever tools they could get at the treasure with. Little did they know, those police deputies were guarding the cache of gold bars.

After the excitement had subsided, and with police deputies still on guard, one gold bar was sent to the University of Florida. Ouch! The bars were not gold at all. The University determined it was not gold, but a bar with alloy metals in it.

The site was found when bulldozers were cleaning out land for a new Department of Health Building. Low and behold, the previous land had a metal producing building on it. The building was long gone and so are the "gold bars". One can only find ¾ of a bar displayed at the courthouse in Fernandina Beach on Center Street.

Gold Bars found in New Fernandina

Figure 10

Gold Bars found in New Fernandina

Figure 11

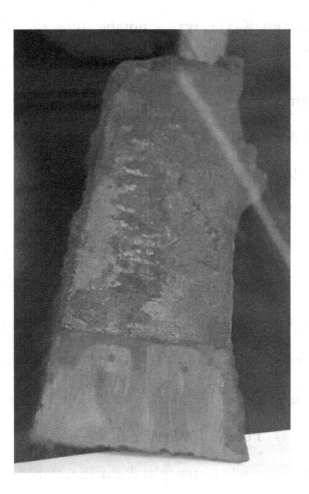

CHAPTER FIVE

Expedition Amelia

IN 1935 T. HOWARD KELLY was a notable literary, novelist, and writer who wrote for several magazines such as: *Esquire*, *McClure's*, *Smart Set* and *Cosmopolitan* magazines. Kelly was an individual who organized the expeditions to the "jungles" of Amelia Island.

His group was looking for Captain William Kidd's treasure, which the privateer had allegedly put several treasures on the island. With Kelly was a group of wealthy adventurers that were looking for Kidd's treasure also. After it was all over, they had an unknown number of expeditions to the island.

Conditions were brutal when looking for Captains Kidd's lost treasure. (They also hunted Aury's treasures). They had no metal detectors to aid in the finding of anything, let alone treasure. There were snakes on the island and they had no spray for all the species of bugs on the island.

The treasure hunters took a survey and a magnetometer and would simply grid out an area. They would use simple tools, shovels, and rakes and dig along the lines. The group hunted multiple locations including two on Egan's Creek, one on Franklintown and one on Talbot Island. Coins were found, but how many remains a mystery. It could have five or fifty-five. The group of gentlemen may have found large chest of treasures, the author does not know; maybe you do? After an unknow number of expeditions on Amelia Island and the twenty previous searches for Blackbeard's treasure by other explorers, we can be sure they found something!

Some coins found by the T. Howard Kelly's Group

Courtesy of the Cloyd Family

Figure 12

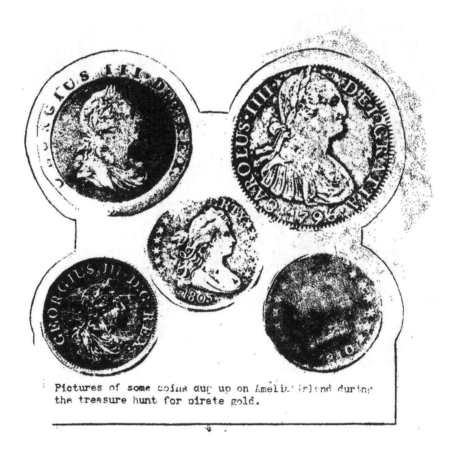

Pictures of some coins dug up on Amelia Island during the treasure hunt for pirate gold.

Coins found on Amelia Island by the author that were identical to the coins in

Figure 12 (The coin in the middle the author determined to be a replica)

Figure 13

T. Howard Kelley pointing to a map of Amelia Island

Courtesy of Donna Cloyd (granddaughter), Travis Cloyd (great-grandson),

and Carissa Cloyd Zillner (great-granddaughter), of T. Howard Kelly

Figure 13.2

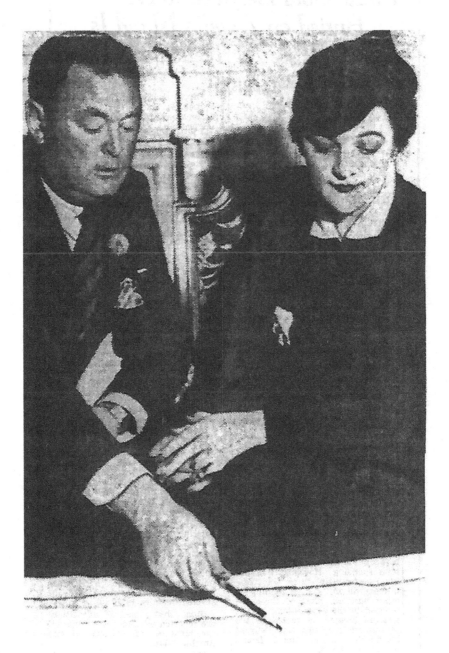

Figure 14. Front page of The Florida Times–Union, 1935

The Florida Times-Union

JACKSONVILLE, FLORIDA, MONDAY, NOVEMBER 25, 1935.

Pirate Gold Believed to Be Buried on Amelia Island Is Lure for Treasure Hunters

T. Howard Kelly, Writer, Is Organizer of Group That Will Make Search.

Pirate gold will lure a group of "gentlemen adventurers" to Amelia Island, where shortly after the first of the year they will begin their quest for the doubloons of buccaneers, who tradition says, found the Barrier Islands off the Northeast Florida coast an excellent hiding place for their loot as early as the latter part of the Seventeenth century.

T. Howard Kelly, noted writer, who calls Fernandina his home, is the organizer of what he calls the Amelia Island Pirate Treasure Expedition, and announced the purpose of the explorations while a visitor here Saturday.

Mr. Kelly said the following prominent persons are interested in the expedition.

Bradshaw Crandell, Cosmopolitan Magazine cover artist; John Charles Thomas, famous baritone; George Angue Dobyne, retired capitalist of Easton, Md., and Palm Beach; Jay Hyde Barnum, noted illustrator for Colliers, American Magazine, Pictorial Review and Cosmopolitan; ____ Kimbark Howell, New London and Palm Beach yachtaman; Robert Ferguson and Carter Carnegie of Cumberland Island, Ga.; George Fenton, Buffalo and Palm Beach sportsman; Bill Berri, New York City and Miami yachtsman; Dan Kelly Jr., legislator and attorney of Fernandina, and others.

Mr. Kelly who divides his time between Florida and the East, has been spending November in the State perfecting plans for the treasure expedition and attending to other business. Most of those interested in the explorations for the treasure became attracted to the venture while visiting Mr. Kelly at his beach house on Amelia Island last Spring, he said.

"From 1683 to 1685, a pirate named Agramont, who became notorious as 'Abraham', plundered, burned and scourged what is now St. Catherine's Island above Sapelo Island, and continued his depredations down to Amelia Island.

Used By Blackbeard.

"Later, in 1715, Thomas Leache, famous as Blackbeard, used the island, now known on the United States maps as Blackbeard Island, for a base. He even extended his operations as far down as Little Talbot Island, using the harbor of Fernandina.

"Luis Aury, another buccaneer, took Amelia Island in 1817, and there tried to establish a republic, after erecting the flag of Mexico.

"Gradually, the section, on account of being close to deep water, became a popular rendezvous for pirates."

The most direct information concerning pirate treasure is connected with the story of Captain Kidd, according to Mr. Kelly. There are residents on Amelia Island today, he related, whose fathers and grandfathers have told them a story of the four expeditions made by the famous buccaneer and his terrorizing marauders, sailing in and out of the harbor at what is now Fernandina.

So the story goes, when Captain Kidd visited Amelia Island on his last trip, he anchored off shore, and sent every member of his crew into the jungle thickets with treasure, which, it is said, they buried in a designated spot.

The narrators of this quaint and exciting lore say that after he had caused the doubloons to be cached, he ordered the majority of his crew killed on the spot, or had them cast overboard at sea. This left only him and his chosen few conspirators with a knowledge of the coveted fortune in pirate gold.

Since that time, 20 expeditions are reported to have made hunts for the treasure of Blackbeard and Amelia Islands.

An article from *The New York American* published on Sunday,

December 22, 1935 written by T. Howard Kelly

Figure 15

Vho Think—SUNDAY, DECEMBER 22, 1935　　　　　　　　　　　　E—3

Buried Pirate Gold Lures Expedition To Amelia Island Jungles Off Florida

Expedition to Hunt Treasure Cached by Capt. Kidd and 17th Century Buccaneers

By T. HOWARD KELLY,

Author of "What Outfit Buddy?" "The Unknown Soldier"—"Lovers' Island"—"Enchanted Dusk," and Other Books and Stories.

SOMETIME within the next few weeks, John Charles Thomas, acting as Commodore of our Amelia Island Pirate Treasure Expedition's yacht fleet, will break out a black and white pirate flag from the signal mast of his flagship Masquerader in the picturesque harbor of Fernandina, Florida.

Thereupon some 20 members of our company of gentlemen adventurers will assemble on the Masquerader's quarterdeck to receive final orders concerning our forthcoming plunge into the almost impenetrable jungles of historic, palm-fringed Amelia Island, which lies just off the northeastern mainland of Florida.

In its tangled thickets of pines, Spanish bayonets, oaks, palmettoes and cabbage palms we will conduct an intensive and systematic search for chests of buccaneer gold and gems which history, tradition and legend maintain were secretly cached there by Agramont, Captain Kidd, Blackbeard, Luis Aury and other cutthroat sea bandits.

victed, and hanged as history relates.

Ever so often the discovery of an anchor chain fastened to an Amelia Island jungle oak is reported. But I am convinced that Kidd did not leave such an obvious marker for his buried treasure. If I am not badly mistaken, Kidd's cache is in the area we intend searching.

About 35 years ago, two Negroes named Goss and Pinkney stumbled across a partly buried iron chest in Amelia's southeastern jungle. It contained approximately $20,000 in 17th and 18th century coins. Pinkney was subsequently reported on the mainland. But Goss dropped out of sight and mysterious stories of tragedy

Hand-Crank milled coins found on Amelia Island

Figure 16

According of Donna Cloyd (granddaughter), Travis Cloyd (great-grandson), and Carissa Cloyd Zillner (great-granddaughter), of T. Howard Kelly, he had been all over the world. In the summer, Kelly would stay at his island house. He died in this house on Amelia Island in 1967 at the age of 72.

Articles not in this Chapter are as follows: *Buried Gold in Florida, Pirate Gold is Believed to be Buried on Amelia Island, Rich Sportsmen to Seek Buried Pirate Gold* and *Sportsmen Plan Treasure Hunt on Amelia Island.* (All in 1935). The articles are identical in content and were not used in this book.

As aforementioned, the stories contained in this publication describe a handful of well-known pirates on the island like Captain William Kidd, Edward Teach, also known as Blackbeard, Agramont, Luis Aury, and many more. These articles have one theme; "Is there treasure on Amelia Island?" Yes, there is. How much is yet to be determined!

CHAPTER SIX

Artifacts & Ocean

BY LAND OR SEA THERE **is** treasure on Amelia Island, Florida; you just have to look for it! I will show you in this chapter the Atlantic Ocean and all its glory. The ocean can be angry with waves taller than houses or it can be flat like a sheet of ice.

As an archaeologist I will explain to you how a Spanish Galleon becomes a shipwreck. A Spanish Galleon can survive a hurricane if they are in deep water (not always but the majority of the time). When the ships skirted the coast and a hurricane or a northeaster hits (remember they did not have weather forecasting at the time) that was when trouble could start.

A fully loaded 1715 Galleon had approximately an 18-foot draft (the draft is the water line of the ship to the bottom of the Galleon) if you have a 35-foot crest (crest is the highest part of the wave) with a trough (trough is the lowest part of the wave) of 19 feet, the ship will hit the bottom and crack like an egg.

The deck would shear off and surf to the shore like a surf board. The bottom would fall where it hit and all was lost. Contained in the ship were ballast stones, silver bars and boxes of silver, gold coins and jewelry.

The authors' group had the chance to go on private property near the Atlantic Ocean and search. Our group found approximately 210 pins, spikes, tacks and miscellaneous items. These items were made of iron and bronze and would be used to hold the ship together. Also discovered were Spanish coins and a French ring made of silver.

Looking at Figure 17 our group excavated these pins, spikes and tacks. This is about 50% of the artifacts we discovered.

Excavated pins, spikes, and tacks found on the South End.

Figure 17

Four spikes, notice the U.S. Quarter to put the size in perspective. Notice

how they are bent by the massive power of the Atlantic Ocean

Figure 17.5

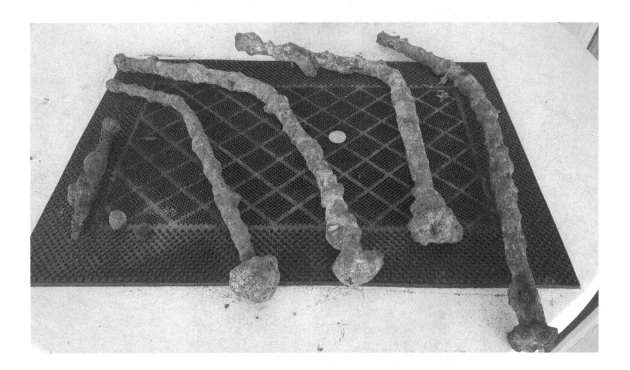

Spikes and pins out of the approximately 210 our group found

Figure 17.6

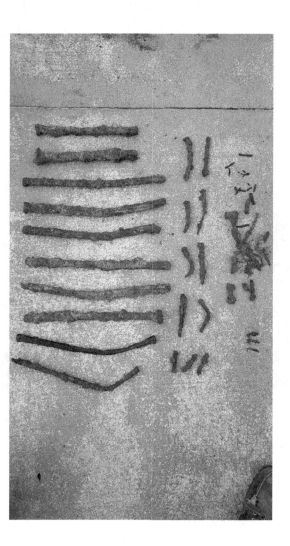

These are the log sheets that the author created to determine

where the pins, spikes, jewelry and coins were located

Figure 18

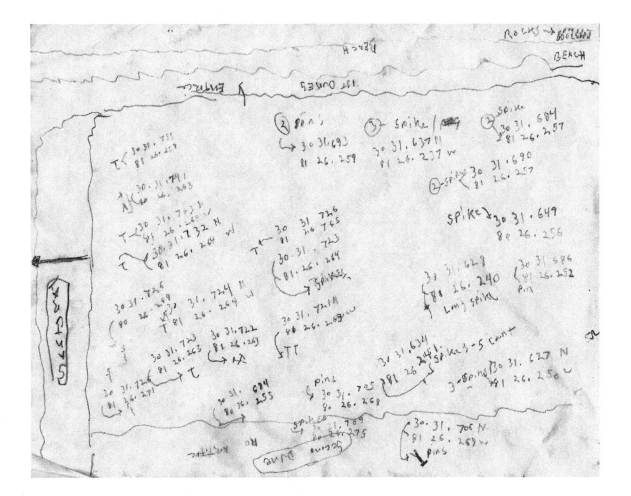

The second log sheet from the South End of Amelia Island

Figure 19

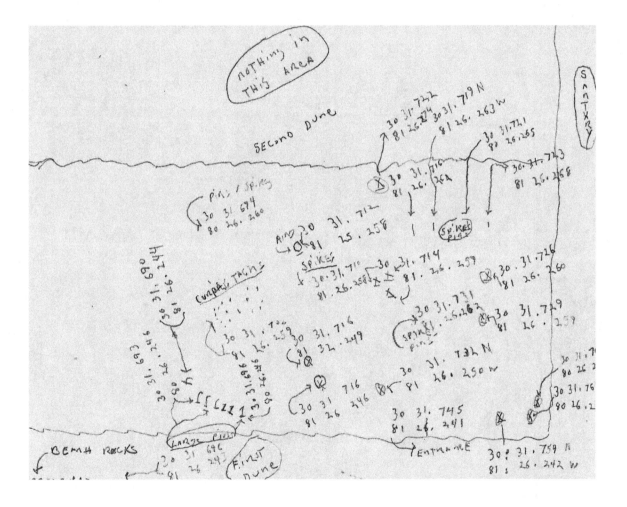

Spanish Coins found on the South End of Amelia Island

Figure 20

This is a small piece of wood with spikes in it, located in

the same area as the coins, spikes, pins and jewelry

Figure 21

A French Ring discovered by our group

Figure 22

The author holds up a coin he excavated

Figure 23

Two Spanish coins found by a member of our team

Figure 24

Figure 25

The author took this picture in 1978. It is of a massive keel that washed in from the beach. The keel runs along the bottom in the center of the ship

Figure 26

Eugene Lyon Ph.D. was a Historian and was the foremost expert of Spanish history in the world. He lived in St Augustine, Florida and was head of the Department of History at Flagler Collage. Dr. Lyon went to the Archives in Seville Spain and found many documentations of possible shipwrecks on the East Coast.

On April 28th 2018, he gave me permission to include some of his documents in *Amelia Island Book of Secrets*. He died shortly thereafter. These are two of his documents.

Figure 27

EUGENE LYON, Ph.D.

April 13, 1994

Please find attached:

1. A report on the two vessels from the 1715 <u>Tierra Firme</u> fleet which were evidently never salvaged, and which may in fact be the source of the coins you have found in your work area.

2. Also sent along is a summary of Florida documents which relate to the 1715 business, one of which describes the trip "north" at some date prior to November, 1715, when one of the Florida Treasury officials, Francisco Menéndez Marquéz, made the voyage to check out the matter. I also examined the Florida accounts (Archives of the Indies[hereinafter AGI] <u>Contaduría</u> 952), but found no entry for the trip.

3. Along with these I send a copy of a document from AGI <u>Consulados</u>, which describes the shipwrecks and the personnel losses on each vessel. I translated the general part and those which refer to the two ships <u>San Miguel</u> and <u>Ciervo.</u>

Since the accounts gave no further clue or evidence, I think the best immediate follow-up for me is to trace the Virginia Governor's story, which implies information arriving in Willamsburg about the north Florida shipwrecks.

This is an exciting business, which may yield some good results. Please advise when and how I can help. With best personal wishes, I am

Yours sincerely,

Eugene Lyon

Figure 28

Report on 1715 Shipwrecks north of St. Augustine

Generally, the locations of the 1715 losses are pretty well known, with some notable exceptions. Unfortunately, no definitive identification has been made on any of the known shipwrecks, but some of the sites are tentatively identified. The early survivors stated that they knew where all the ships had wrecked except for four; the Concepción, the San Miguel, the French prize and the Grifon. This is so stated by the chief pilot of Ubilla's fleet, Captain Nicolás de Ynda, in a letter dated from Havana on 16 August 1715 and found in AGI Santo Domingo 419. As we know, Grifon escaped to return safely to France. Up to the date of that report, the survivors always had said the ships were ten leagues (almost 35 n.m. apart, @ 3.44 n.m. to a league), lying from 27 d. 15' to 27 d 50'. After that point, they said the wrecks were 15 or 16 leagues apart. You can only add those extra leagues to the north, for the southernmost of the wrecks was clearly Miguel de Lima's urca, the Santísima Trinidad. This designation of Lima's ship as the southernmost site never changed during the years of Spanish salvage up to 1719, when effective work on the sites ceased.

On the north end of the known wrecks immediately after the hurricane ceased, the New Spain Almiranta was located at 27 d 50', almost precisely the location of the Cabin Wreck. That shipwreck has yielded the type of coins (Mexico mint)and the kind of personal and religious jewelry and artifacts one might expect to come from that vessel. Moreover, it is quite logical that the other New Spain capital ship, the Capitana, was lost ca. two leagues to the south. This corresponds with the "Corrigan's" site. In fact, the testimony of one Pedro de la Vega makes it certain that the Almiranta of Ubilla's fleet and its camp were located north of that of his Capitana, for as the English raiders came down upon the latter camp, Spaniards fled southward along the beach. Again, the type of material found there, with a New Spain provenience, would correspond with a large, passenger-carrying capital vessel from Vera Cruz. It is evident, moreover, that the salvage camp of the patache of New Spain was located some distance to the southward of the two New Spain capital ships, since one observer, Pedro de la Vega, required the time from 7 p.m. to 3 a.m. to arrive at the patache camp(Testimony of Pedro de la Vega, AGI Escribanía de Cámara 55-C, fol. 111vto.), which in turn was located some two leagues to the north of the southernmost of the New Spain shipwreck sites, that of the ship of Miguel de Lima.Lima himself says that his ship was "the first, which is towards the upper Keys (from the rest)" (AGI Santo Domingo 419).

This leaves the Concepción, a few survivors of which came ashore on raft somewhere north of the Sebastian inlet, and the San Miguel and the Ciervo. It is easy to confuse the two ships which bore the name of San Miguel. It is evident that the lost one was the larger vessel, which had sailed all the way from Spain with Echevers, and its data follows:

San Miguel

A frigate, Vizcayan built. 180 3/4 tons; 22 cannons, 18 4-pounders and 4 two-pounders. Her beam was 22.5', her keel length 72', and her overall length was 83'.. Master is Joesph Coyto de Melo; he was among the sixty two persons drowned as the ship was lost with all hands. Also included in the lost personnel were Don Domingo and Don Tomás Moynos, citizens of Cádiz, Don Joseph Tamorlan, Guardian Jacome de Noblería, Pilot Alonso de Silvestre and Quartermaster Domingo de Yguzquiza. 22 sailors, 24 grommets and four pages were lost. Not to be confused with another San Miguel, a sloop prize captured by Echeverz in the Caribbean and likely disposed of in Havana. The larger San Miguel may be the vessel reported lost north of St. Augustine. She carried tobacco from Havana and was a "registry" vessel, evidently from Cádiz; that is, it had special permission for lading by merchants from that city.

Remember when the author told you that the deck shears off and surfs to the shore? That is exactly what this ship has done. What is the age of this ship? The age could be from the 1600s to the 1800s, however, with that being said, the Spanish coins and jewelry found on the site tend to suggest it is a Spanish ship in origin.

Spikes, pins, coins and jewelry can only mean one thing; a shipwreck. I surmise that these could be the shipwrecks of the *San Miguel* or the *Ciervo*. These ships sank in the 1715 Plate Fleet. (Plate means **treasure**).

So, what does this all mean? It means, in my opinion, that there is at least one (or more) Colonial Period (1607 to 1776) shipwreck's in the Nassau Sound or International waters. The evidence supports this theory that shipwrecks are in this area.

This map was drawn by Lou Ullian of the *Real Eight Company* in the 1960's and 1970's from memory. Graciously, I have permission to use this map by Helen Ullian and Rex Stocker, the surviving members of the company.

The *Real Eight Company* was the first company to find and salvage Spanish shipwrecks on the coast of Florida and eventually they came to Amelia Island. On Amelia Island, they found many gold and silver coins. On Talbot Island there were even more coins. Here is Lou Ullian's Map of Amelia and Talbot Island..

Figure 29

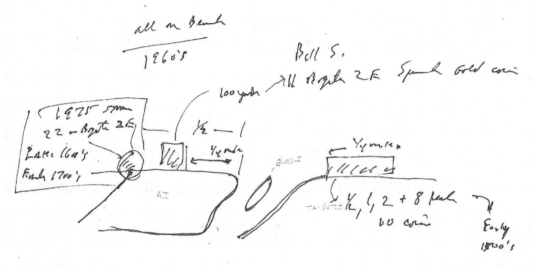

Lou Ullian's handwritten map shows where the *Real Eight Company* found treasure on the beach and in the Atlantic Ocean.

<u>Amelia Island Florida in 1960's.</u>

11 Bogotá 2 Escudos Spanish (gold) Coins

<u>Talbot Island Florida</u>

10 Spanish Reales (silver) Coins

Early 1500's

1531-1540's

<u>Amelia Island in 1975</u>

22 Bogota 2 Escudos Spanish (gold coins)

Early 1600's

Early 1700's

The author has worked on one primary research vessel called the *Polly-L* for 20 years, and it is the most spectacular archaeological platform in the world.

It was constructed through private investors to investigate and hunt treasure in the waters off Amelia Island. Warren Lokey was a primary investor of the research vessel. His mother Polly Lokey had a terrible accident in Cozumel, Mexico and was on the way to the hospital when she died.

The President of the *Amelia Research & Recover Company*, Doug Pope, proposed an idea that they name the vessel after Warrens mother. He accepted; he wanted to memorialize his mother (she was a waitress and her patrons called her Polly-L) and the vessel was named the *Polly-L*. Warren died a few years later but his mother's name still lives on.

The *Polly-L* the best Archaeological platform in the world

Figure 29.2

The author coming out of the Atlantic Ocean with

dive gear one mile off of Amelia Island

Figure 29.5

Colonial Period coin found by the author

Figure 29.6

CHAPTER SEVEN

Witches and Giants of Amelia Island

Witches

THE OLD-TIMERS CALLED IT ALICE Island; a member from our group and I were driving around and he asked me if I ever heard of the island. He said it was by the Amelia Island Airport; my response to his question was: "Are you talking about Crane Island?"

The old-timers called the island Alice, but it was actually named Crane Island. The island had been disputed for decades by developers and conservationists. After changing owners several times, a compromise was obtained. It was developed, not on the scale the owners wanted, but that is what comprise is about.

The island's namesake was Sarah Alice and people called her a witch.

After her father died and her sister moved off the island to get married, she was alone. The people I spoke with said she was not a witch. They just used those stories to frighten their children to not trespass on the island or to keep their behaviors in line.

Sarah Alice (and her sister Esther Silva) inherited the house that her father built. Sarah lived off the grid with no gas or electricity. She rarely left her island home and would only trek the few miles to New Fernandina every few months.

In 1952 disaster struck! Sarah's house was in flames. Nothing was left but the fireplace and the well for water. There are many versions of why her house burned to the ground. Some say she committed suicide, which would be unlikely as bones aren't easy to burn (even in a cremation they need to grind the teeth and bone shards to turn them into dust).

Others think she just packed up and left. Why would she do that? Sarah loved her piece of paradise (so, I am told). I find it unlikely. So, where did she go?

As stated, no bones were found at the scene of the fire and no evidence was found to support these theories. The next theory states that she was murdered for her gold and silver and tossed in the river; I can accept this possibility. They have not found any bones and the land now has mostly been developed.

House Burned

Figure 30

Cover of the Fernandina Beach News-Leader
on Nov 14th, 1952

The author standing by the well on Crane Island, before development

Figure 31

Close-up of Well

Figure 32

Brick from the Fireplace

Figure 33

A Brick found in the Well

Figure 34

Cauldron

Figure 35

We will probably never know what happed to Sarah Alice on the night she went missing. Her bones have never been found, but maybe one day they will!

Giants!

On Amelia Island there are many shell middens, but few burial mounds. Middens are trash piles and mounds are used for burials. (Hence the term burial mounds). There are over fifty middens and mounds that have been found on the island, but most are gone now. (Timucuan Indians Mounds).

Relic hunters, housing developments and land archaeologists have destroyed most of the burial mounds. Walkers Mound, Lighthouse Mound, and Harrison's Homestead are some of the burial mounds on Amelia Island. The Lighthouse Mound was completely destroyed in an archaeological excavation.

In regards to the Harrison's Homestead Burial Mound, and on behalf of the Smithsonian Institute, Scientist Augustus Mitchell M.D. found several remains including a giant skeleton. It had double rows of teeth; seven feet tall (over seven feet tall was a giant at that time) with a huge battle-axe. Could this be true?

The Article from *Some Human Skeleton Remains from Amelia Island,* seems to verify at least part of the story. In 1848 this mound was excavated. The mound was 15 feet in height, 30 feet in diameter; they put a 4-foot trench down the middle of the mound.

Found in the mound by Mitchell was "The largest stone axe that I have ever seen". Next, he found the largest skull in the mound it was in perfect condition for two hours then it disintegrated (due to the exposure to oxygen) into small pieces (Bullen, 79-80).

So, is this real? Absolutely! However, that being said, the giant did not have two rows of teeth, two smaller skeletons had two and three rows of teeth. Mitchell calculated by the decaying bones, that the skeleton was seven feet tall or larger. So, he was considered an actual giant! (For the time period).

❧ CHAPTER EIGHT ❧

❧ CHAPTER EIGHT ❧

Drive

IMAGINE DRIVING IN THE EARLY 1900's from the North End of Amelia Island to the South End of the island. With the completion of 14th Street, taking you to Old Fernandina (now identified as Old Town) in the early 1800's, what would you see?

Picture this tour in your mind; I will take you, the reader on an amazing journey, so let's get started. In Old Town (Old Fernandina) you would see the remnants of Fort San Carlos that was completed in 1816. It was built over a native Timucuan village.

Before 14th street was constructed the only way to get from Old Fernandina was by boat or by a pier constructed to reach New Fernandina.

As stated in Chapter 3, Old Town (Old Fernandina) was a haven for treasure. Many treasures have been found in Old Town and the surrounding areas.

According to *Seeing Fernandina,* while traveling south and .04 mile from American Beach, you will arrive at the site of the Harrison Plantation. Simply turn right at this location, and one can visit this historical site... sadly the Plantation was burned down by Federal Troops during the Civil War in 1836.

In the side yard was an ancient well. On the left side of the house were the family plots (burial grounds). The Harrison family, upon learning of the approaching Federal troops, buried all their treasures and fled the island. When they returned, they could not find the spot where the treasure was located! The treasure was never found.

Continuing 1.4 miles from American Beach to the south turn right to Walkers Landing, tabby remains are thought to be the foundations of a Seminary established in the late 1690's for the training of priests. The English slaughtered the priests in 1702 (City Commission, 43).

According to a *Report*, (Unknown Author), in 1938 they had few roads and the further south you drove, the rougher the roads became. They were exceedingly narrow with high and low sand dunes. There were few turnabouts and the dunes were overgrown with scrubs.

The curves were horrendous, and the drivers were advised to proceed with caution as several Indian mounds were in the vicinity. The area was asserted to have been the site of much buried pirate treasure during the Buccaneer and Privateers' days.

Continuing from Walker's Fish Camp, a treacherous sand road rises sharply. Reaching the crest of the dune there is a view of the beach for many miles north and south. Talbot Island is visible across the Nassau Sound (1980. Page 34).

This was Amelia Island in 1938, currently it has been developed. Not an empty lot to be found, existing homes are being torn down and new mansion-sized homes are being built.

It is not the quaint island it once was; it has turned into a massive resort island. That being said, it is still a wonderful place that I am proud to live in!

⚜ CHAPTER NINE ⚞

Finally......X Marks The Spot

IN THE PAST CHAPTERS WE have explored the location of Amelia Island, a brief history of the island, and Pirates. In addition to Old Fernandina / New Fernandina, Expedition Amelia, the Atlantic Ocean and the artifacts found on the island; Witches and Giants, "Driven" through the Island, and finally....X Marks the Spot.

When researching the context of this publication, Chapters 3-9 have been about treasure lost and found on Amelia Island. There are many rumors (some with high probability) of treasures that have been found in the last twenty years on the Amelia Island beaches.

For example, a gentleman who found nineteen gold coins by a resort on the island, and the beach patrol who found two gold coins on our shores. Friends of friends who often can't provide the coins or evidence of such claimed treasures. So, goes the story, legend, and history of Amelia Island; fact vs fiction!

You don't need to be a professional treasure hunter to find treasure!

Figure 36

So, it's time to purchase a beach metal detector and comb the beaches of Amelia Island. You will find treasures; it just takes patience and an understanding of this rich Island's history. Look at Figure 36 with all the treasure in a box; these were found by the author located in eight months.

Treasure to some people is a shark's tooth. To other people, artifacts, jewelry, silver or gold is their dream. Some say the island itself is a jewel. All can be found on Amelia Island, Florida. Is there treasure on this island? Absolutely!!!!

REFERENCES CITED

Amelia Island Museum of History. The Historic Splendor of Amelia
Island, Fernandina Beach, Florida. Amelia Island Museum of History.
1997

Bellen, Adelaide. Some Human-Skeletal Remains from Amelia Island
Florida. University of Florida. 1973

Buried Pirate Gold Lures Expedition to Amelia Island Jungles off Florida
The New York American, Sunday, December 22,1935

Buried Gold in Florida, The New York Times
May 28, 1897.

Fernandina Chamber of Commerce
Unpublished Letter February 3, 1934

Documents, The Maritime Museum of Amelia Island Archives, 1935.

Discovery of Gold Near Fernandina, News-Leader
October 31, 1928.

Fairbanks, Charles H, and Jerald T Mcanich
Florida Archaeology, Academic Press. Orlando, Florida. 1918.

Gooding, William. Fort Clinch Manuscript distributed by The Florida
Department of Natural Resources, State Parks Division. Fernandina
Beach Florida. 1974.

Lyon, Eugene, Personal Communication. 2018.

Jaccard, Lawrance D. Indians of Amelia Island, Lexington Ventures Inc. Fernandina Beach, Florida. 2000.

Johannes, Jan. Yesterday's Reflections, (Preface) Lexington Ventures Inc. Fernandina Beach, Florida. 2000.

Map. The Martine Museum of Amelia Island Archives, Fernandina Beach, Florida. 1960.

Measuring Worth. 2006. Accessed 2020. <http://www:measuringworth.html>

Morison, Samuel. The European Discovery of America. Oxford University Press. New York. 1974.

Olexer, Barbara. The Enslavement of the American Indian in Colonial Joyous Publishing. 2005.

Pirate Gold is Believe to Be Buried on Amelia Island is Lure for Treasure Hunters Cover, The Florida Times–Union, November 29, 1935.

Ralph D. Paine. The Book of Pirates Treasures: London: Heinemann. 1911.

Report unknown author or publisher, manuscript on file. The Maritime Museum of Amelia Island Archives, Fernandina Beach, Florida. 1980's

Scott, Thomas M. Environmental Geology Series: Jacksonville Sheet. Florida Bureau of Geology Map Series No. 89. Tallahassee, Florida.

Sportsmen Plan Treasure Hunt in South Isles. The New York Times December 16, 1935.

Rich Sportsmen to Seek Buried Pirate Gold, Tampa Morning Tribute, November 25, 1935.

The City Commission of Fernandina. <u>Seeing Fernandina.</u> American Guide Series. 1940.

Woodard, Colin. <u>The Republic of Pirates</u>, Harcourt, Inc. 2007.

<u>Unknown Text</u> unknown publisher or author page. (Partial Text). The Maritime Museum of Amelia Island Archives, Amelia Island, Fernandina Beach. 1950's

Ullian, Lou, Personal conversation with Rex Stocker and Helen Ullian. 2020.

The Photos and Illustration pages follow. The author has taken thousands of photos on Amelia Island. Photos of treasure that I cannot show you. If the reader ever gets a chance to visit and explore Amelia Island you will not be disappointed!

PHOTOS & ILLUSTRATIONS

The Moon photographed off my deck on Amelia Island

Figure 37

APPRECIATION PAGE

Thanks to the *News-Leader* for allowing the author permission to use two news articles.

Thanks to the *Fernandina Chamber of Commerce* for allowing the author to use an unpublished letter.

Thanks to *The Florida Times-Union* for permission to use an article published in 1935.

Thanks to Donna Cloyd (granddaughter), Travis Cloyd (great-grandson), and Carissa Cloyd Zillner (great-granddaughter), of T. Howard Kelly for allowing me to use his photos.

Special thanks to William L. Taylor, for putting our group on the location on the South End (with permission).

Thanks to Helen Ullian and Rex Stocker for allowing the author to use Lou's map.

Extra Special Thanks to Noël Lehman and Pixi-Pocket for being my encouragement and muses!

INDEX